MW01717023

*Storms come and go
but grace is forever.*

Roger Allen Cook

Sailing by Grace

A Journey of the Heart

Roger Allen Cook

Sailing by Grace
by Roger Allen Cook

Published by GBC Media
12501 Telegraph, Taylor, MI 48180
Web site: www.GBCmedia.com

Printed in the United States of America

ISBN 0-9707780-0-7
Library of Congress Card Number: 2001116026

Interior and cover design by Kimberly D'Angelo at Bookcovers.com

Cover art: Moonlit Sails by Charles Vickery used with permission of Clipper Ship Gallery, 116 N. Whittaker, New Buffalo, MI 49117

Acknowledgements

With deepest appreciation to my wife Konnie and my children Jonathan, Matthew, Andrew, and Elizabeth. My gratitude to Mariah Humphries, Sherry Dady, Donna Herring, Tom and Cindy Downs, Jim and Deb Hill, Joe and Winnie Guthrie, and all those who inspired and encouraged this work and provided the wise counsel and expertise to make it a reality. My thanks to Kimberly D'Angelo and Bookcovers.com for their wonderful work and to the Clipper Ship Gallery for their permission to use a Charles Vickery work on the cover. I send a special thanks to my parents Floyd and Ludie Cook. Alzheimer's disease has robbed Mom of the ability to enjoy this volume, but her love for the Lord and His Word was deeply ingrained in her younger years and I am sure that her communion with Him is now in words that could never be written with mortal pen.

Table of Contents

Introduction

I have always been fascinated with sailing ships as they challenge the elements on the high seas. The feeling of adventure must at times be both exhilarating and fearful. Many artists have made marine art their specialty by capturing the experience of these great ships on canvas. The beauty and gracefulness of blue-sky sailing gives one the sense of speed and freedom while the action of angry waters show us danger and determination. In our journey of life we face conditions similar to these great ships. Life can be smooth and gentle with the wind filling our sails or stormy and turbulent with a contrary wind and a hindering tide. The constant factor in the changing environmental conditions of our lives is the grace of God. God's grace is available to us in any and every situation and circumstance. I pray that these inspirational thoughts will be a blessing to you as you chart your course through life on a daily basis. Just a few minutes with the Lord and His word will make a great difference. There is no reason for anyone to experience the journey unaided, when you could be sailing by grace.

Roger Allen Cook
December, 2000

Grace

Sailing by Grace
Authored by Grace
Intervening Grace
The River of Grace
One Drop of Grace
By His Grace
The Well of Grace
Through the Eyes of Grace
I Belong to Grace
Greater Grace
The Harbor of Psalm 51
The Hand of Grace
Graceful Breezes

Sailing by Grace

It is glorious to know that in the midst of the storm, when our soul is melted because of trouble, the One who rules the wind and waves stands near. He guides us to the quietness of our desired haven. Sailing by grace allows us to cherish the journey of life.

I think of life as a voyage,
A great sailing ship at sea,
Sails filled with potential
To move at the Master's decree.

We are sailors by His call
At times the wind in our face
With Jesus as our Captain
We know we're sailing by grace.

Watching the horizon ahead
And navigating by the Word,
Even in the noise of living
The still small voice is heard.

At times the sailing is rough
When the storms blow strong,
And decisions must be made,
Sometimes they are wrong.

Yet He is always right there
Giving guidance from above,
While redirecting our journey
And revealing His great love.

Sometimes sailing is smooth
With seas unusually calm;
Time to reflect on His love
And meditate on a Psalm.

The sailor must be diligent
To check the charts each day,
Reviewing compass settings,
Resisting the desire to stray.

Whether storm tossed and torn
By powerful winds and waves,
Or floating in gentle breezes
We know that Jesus saves.

We seek that port of entry
Never from there to roam,
The refuge He calls Heaven,
That harbor we call home.

You need not sail unaided.
Give Jesus His rightful place,
And through the seas of life
You will be sailing by Grace.

21 Oh that men would praise the LORD for his goodness,
and for his wonderful works to the children of men! 22 And
let them sacrifice the sacrifices of thanksgiving, and declare
his works with rejoicing. 23 They that go down to the sea in
ships, that do business in great waters; 24 These see the
works of the LORD, and his wonders in the deep. 25 For he
commandeth, and raiseth the stormy wind, which lifteth up
the waves thereof. 26 They mount up to the heaven, they go
down again to the depths: their soul is melted because of
trouble. 27 They reel to and fro, and stagger like a drunken
man, and are at their wit's end. 28 Then they cry unto the
LORD in their trouble, and he bringeth them out of their
distresses. 29 He maketh the storm a calm, so that the waves
thereof are still. 30 Then are they glad because they be quiet;
so he bringeth them unto their desired haven.
Psalm 107:21~30

Authored by Grace

Have you considered how the story of your life would read in book form, especially of it were written by someone who knew it as well as you do? Remember, each decision is a step in the journey that is your life. With Jesus as your Editor-in-chief, the resulting story will be an eternal best seller.

A story of life is unfolding
With events occurring each day,
The continuing story of my life
From a babe to hairs of gray.

God is moving my hand to write
A journal of my walk on earth,
Page upon page of decisions,
Of fear and sorrow and mirth.

He helps me pick up the pen
And lays His great hand over mine,
Teaching me to write in His will
With strokes so artful and fine.

A mystically wonderful saga
Of a life lived in time and space,
This diary of daily living,
One that is authored by grace.

Like a child who is learning
To write the language of school,
Help from the master's hand
Gives guidance in using the tool.

I, like the child appreciate
The initial aid of His hand
But soon strive to be free and
Independent whenever I can.

Grace

Desiring to write by myself
A story line authored by me,
With choices that I get to make
About new chapters yet to be.

Looking back on my journal
I can see each twist and turn,
And the times I wrote on my own
The hard lessons I had to learn.

Jesus, take control of my hand
As I write the rest of my days.
Guide the choice of each letter
Each word, sentence, and phrase.

Let the conclusion of the matter
Show Your hand set in place,
Writing the drama of my life,
One that was authored by grace.

1 Wherefore seeing we also are compassed about with so great a cloud of witnesses, let us lay aside every weight, and the sin which doth so easily beset us, and let us run with patience the race that is set before us, 2 Looking unto Jesus the author and finisher of our faith; who for the joy that was set before him endured the cross, despising the shame, and is set down at the right hand of the throne of God.
Hebrews 12:1-2

Intervening Grace

Have you come to a place in your life where all options are gone, and there is not a thing you can do about it? You have a heavenly advocate in the person of Jesus Christ who loves to intervene in your circumstances of life with His grace. With help like that, who would want to stand alone?

The parties were at great odds,
The issues seemed so immense,
To say no deal was possible
Made perfectly good sense.

The defaults were enormous
As were violations of the law,
Audits and examinations
Exposed each and every flaw.

Judgment seemed in order
With punishment put in place,
Then my Lord stepped between
With His intervening grace.

My sin, that was the problem—
Its size and such great extent
My only hope is His mercy
Freely given when I repent.

I knelt physically and in heart
My face stained with tears,
For a life flagrantly soiled
Thru many wandering years.

My advocate presented a plea
A personally guaranteed truce
That would satisfy the debt
From sin turning me loose.

Grace

As forgiveness began to flow
I felt close beneath the wing
Christ's sacrifice paid the price,
Grace became my covering.

His death in place of mine—
What a wondrous thought!
In the shedding of His blood
Salvation has been wrought.

Now there is wonderful peace
Where fear formerly reigned.
Intervening grace has won
And heaven has been gained.

8 If we say that we have no sin, we deceive ourselves, and the
truth is not in us. 9 If we confess our sins, he is faithful and
just to forgive us our sins, and to cleanse us from all
unrighteousness. 10 If we say that we have not sinned, we
make him a liar, and his word is not in us. 1 My little
children, these things write I unto you, that ye sin not.
And if any man sin, we have an advocate with the Father,
Jesus Christ the righteous: 2 And he is the propitiation for
our sins: and not for ours only, but also for the sins of the
whole world.

I John 1:8-2:2

The River of Grace

God says come to the river of grace and it will meet your every need. If you are thirsty come to the Savior and ask for the water of life.

I have heard of a mighty river
Flowing out from God's throne.
A great and powerful torrent
That for our sins does atone.

Washing away transgressions,
Putting Christ in our place,
This flowing cleansing flood,
God's wonderful river of grace.

It moves from the heart of God
And washes us white as snow.
Cleans the soul through Jesus
Who by faith we can know.

Children of a gracious King
Do many times fall and fail
And show fleshly weakness,
Wills so desperately frail.

Some would say of this river
Our sin can hinder its flow,
For grace must have a limit
How far can His patience go.

Pile up the sin of the ages,
The evil arrange in a heap,
God's mighty river of grace
Over all of it will sweep.

Grace

It is required of a sinner
To consider life sin- cursed,
Gather the pieces together
Dive into the river heart first.

His mercy, it will never fail
As our trust in Him we place.
Finding rest and peace upon
God's eternal river of grace.

1 And he showed me a pure river of water of life, clear as
crystal, proceeding out of the throne of God and of the
Lamb. 2 In the midst of the street of it, and on either side of
the river, was there the tree of life, which bare twelve
manner of fruits, and yielded her fruit every month: and
the leaves of the tree were for the healing of the nations. 3
And there shall be no more curse: but the throne of God and
of the Lamb shall be in it; and his servants shall serve him:
4 And they shall see his face; and his name shall be in their
foreheads. 5 And there shall be no night there; and they
need no candle, neither light of the sun; for the Lord God
giveth them light: and they shall reign for ever and ever. 17
And the Spirit and the bride say, Come. And let him that
heareth say, Come. And let him that is athirst come. And
whosoever will, let him take the water of life freely.
Revelation 22:1-5,17

One Drop of Grace

There are toxins that are so potent that only one drop can be fatal to many. There are certain medicines that the smallest dose can save a life. The grace of God is a divine balm that produces eternal results when applied to the life of an individual. Ask God to give you a special touch of grace today so that your every step and your every thought will be pleasing to Him.

When the landscape of the soul,
Withers like an arid plain,
Longing for a gentle shower
Of the Savior's graceful rain

One drop of His loving grace
Provides oceans of relief
Flowering the barren fields
With beauty beyond belief.

Soaking within His presence,
A sobering and humbling time,
When we focus on the Creator
New insights we always find.

Some have not experienced,
The forgiveness of all sin.
And have never opened up,
To invite the Savior within.

They don't know the power of
Just one small drop of grace,
That can cleanse a man inside
And a new heart set in place.

Oh Jesus I need You this day,
To help me win the race
By fueling a worshipful heart
With just one drop of grace.

[26] When the heaven is shut up, and there is no rain, because they have sinned against thee; yet if they pray toward this place, and confess thy name, and turn from their sin, when thou dost afflict them; [27] Then hear thou from heaven, and forgive the sin of thy servants, and of thy people Israel, when thou hast taught them the good way, wherein they should walk; and send rain upon thy land, which thou hast given unto thy people for an inheritance.
II Chronicles 6:26&27

By His Grace

By grace we experienced His love and forgiveness. By grace we walk the path He deems best. By grace we show His love to others. By grace He leads us home.

When I was a broken thing
He became my offering
Covering over everything by His grace

Then He took me by the hand
Gave me strength and helped me stand
Safe in His eternal plan by His grace

When my heart was on the run
And my life was all undone,
Victory was completely won by His grace

Now each day His Word I read
All its wisdom try to heed
As each step the Spirit leads by His grace

One day soon the call will come
We will meet with Him as one
Eternal life is just begun by His grace

Then we will be face to face
With the Son who took our place
Helping us to win the race by His grace

8 For by grace are ye saved through faith; and that not of yourselves: it is the gift of God: 9 Not of works, lest any man should boast.
Ephesians 2:8~9

The Well of Grace

God's provision of grace comes from an inexhaustible supply that cannot adequately be described in earthly terms. We will spend eternity mining the depths of grace and never find its limits. Since it is available now, we might as well start digging.

I went to drink from a fountain
And found it had run dry
I wanted to draw from a well
"No water!" was my cry.

There was an expectation
To quench my nagging thirst
Yet before that can be done
A source must be found first.

My heart desires a spring
To cleanse it deep within
With God's everlasting water
Allowing new life to begin.

There is a spiritual fountain
That flows from the well of grace.
It floods my soul with blessing
And my thirst it does erase.

This well of God's own grace
Flows from the heavenly mountain
Available to whosoever will
My Jesus—He is the fountain.

This provision for my soul—
Such a wonderful well of grace—
Was made available at Calvary
When the Savior took my place.

Are you thirsty for this water
To satisfy the need of your soul?
Allow its healing provision
To wash you and make you whole.

Come to God's well of grace
Through Jesus and you will see
That the flow of living water
Will be there through eternity.

*11 The woman saith unto him, Sir, thou hast nothing to
draw with, and the well is deep: from whence then hast thou
that living water? 12 Art thou greater than our father
Jacob, which gave us the well, and drank thereof himself,
and his children, and his cattle? 13 Jesus answered and said
unto her, Whosoever drinketh of this water shall thirst
again: 14 But whosoever drinketh of the water that I shall
give him shall never thirst; but the water that I shall give
him shall be in him a well of water springing up into
everlasting life.*
John 4:11-14

Through the Eyes of Grace

How quickly we jump to conclusions about someone's actions or attitudes and become judgmental. Since God has so graciously forgiven us of every sin through His Son Jesus Christ, it seems that our gratitude should be demonstrated in our reactions to others. Forgiven sinners ought to be people who are eager and ready to forgive the failures of others. Getting bent out of shape at the smallest offense will not be a characteristic of one who has abundantly received mercy and grace.

The Father was looking down one day,
At all of us in the human race.
His view was one of compassion,
Looking through the eyes of grace.

I will send them My salvation,
It will be packaged within My Son.
His death will pay for their sin,
For a Savior, He's the only One.

Hereafter My view is optional,
Whether as a judge or a father,
Forgiving all those who will call,
Condemning all who don't bother.

When Jesus has entered the picture
And every bit of sin does erase,
God watches my life continually
With only the eyes of grace.

I am not even close to perfect,
He of all knows that very fact
And patiently and firmly corrects
Each and every rebellious act.

Now where is this story going
And what is there here to learn?
How God looks at my actions,
Shows me something to discern.

His kindness in my weakness
Is offered to a repentant heart,
With the grace of understanding
I receive a brand new start.

As I consider the life of others
And the stress upon their face,
Surely I must view my brother,
Looking through the eyes of grace.

*4 They say unto him, Master, this woman was taken in
adultery, in the very act. 5 Now Moses in the law com-
manded us, that such should be stoned: but what sayest
thou? 6 This they said, tempting him, that they might have
to accuse him. But Jesus stooped down, and with his finger
wrote on the ground, as though he heard them not. 7 So
when they continued asking him, he lifted up himself, and
said unto them, He that is without sin among you, let him
first cast a stone at her. 8 And again he stooped down, and
wrote on the ground. 9 And they which heard it, being
convicted by their own conscience, went out one by one,
beginning at the eldest, even unto the last: and Jesus was
left alone, and the woman standing in the midst.*
John 8:4-9

I Belong to Grace

On a recent shopping trip to an antique mall, I was amazed at the prices people wanted for what I considered old junk. There were many items I recognized from my past that I, or my family, had owned and had simply discarded years ago. Yet here they were with a claim of substantial value. I guess you have to be able to see past the problems of the condition of an item and recognize its intrinsic value. I am sure glad God did that with my life. How about you? God certainly has the ability to see through all our sin and rebellion to the intrinsic value of the soul.

Wandering through a bazaar,
Searching for a lost treasure,
Hoping to find a bargain,
To purchase with pleasure.

Just a time of amusement,
Limited by all the detail,
Modest budget constraints
Prevent purchase at retail.

I noticed a beat up trinket,
Bumped and twisted a bit,
Not worth the asking price,
Maybe a penny, that was it.

I thought of increased value,
If fractures could be knit,
Straightened and repaired
And presented visually fit.

My heart was once all alone,
Diminished in value by sin,
Set aside on the sale rack,
Hoping to be bought again.

Who would pay full price,
For goods hopelessly marred,
By the lifestyle of the world,
Inwardly and outwardly scarred.

In came the Prince of grace,
Whose Father is the King.
He wanted my heart for His own,
Full payment He did bring.

So now I belong to grace,
Redeemed by the blood of the Lamb,
Not broken and ruined by sin,
His forgiven child I am.

Repurchased at face value,
Renewed and restored inside,
Living in the land of grace,
Forever with Him to abide.

12 *That we should be to the praise of his glory, who first*
trusted in Christ.
13 *In whom ye also trusted, after that ye heard the word of truth, the gospel of your salvation: in whom also after that ye believed, ye were sealed with that holy Spirit of promise,*
14 *Which is the earnest of our inheritance until the redemption of the purchased possession, unto the praise of his glory.*

Ephesians 1:12-14

Greater Grace

When it comes to grace, Julia H. Johnston put it this way. "Grace, Grace, God's Grace, Grace that will pardon and cleanse within, Grace, Grace, God's Grace, Grace that is greater than all our sin!" Is this true in your life today?

They say Your grace is greater,
Often singing it in a song.
But they don't know my sin,
The things that I do wrong.

I attempt to understand it
What it means to let You forgive,
I feel I should straighten out
The ways in which I live.

If the repairs can be done
And proper corrections made,
Then I can stand before You
With some of my debts paid.

Yet as I consider the matter,
My failures of every kind,
I see the depths of the problem,
And relief I cannot find.

The situation seemed hopeless.
In no way could I meet the test
Of the righteousness of God
And the way I know is best.

When I am totally humbled
By the hold of sin on my heart
Your Spirit says to my soul.
"How about a brand new start?"

I have a special spiritual balm
That covers sin, every trace
When applied to a broken heart
It's the stuff that I call grace.

Paid for by the death of Jesus,
The only One that was pure.
He made My grace available,
For all sin it is the cure.

Yes My grace is greater
Greater than all your sin.
Open your heart by faith,
Abundantly I will pour it in.

[12] Wherefore, as by one man sin entered into the world, and death by sin; and so death passed upon all men, for that all have sinned: [20] Moreover the law entered, that the offence might abound. But where sin abounded, grace did much more abound: [21] That as sin hath reigned unto death, even so might grace reign through righteousness unto eternal life by Jesus Christ our Lord.
Romans 5:12,20~21

The Harbor of Psalm Fifty-One

When we come to a place of honesty with God, like David did, we find peace and rest in His forgiveness. Why is it that we wait so long to sail into the harbor of Psalm 51? Read it today and visit it often.

The storm had long been brewing
The ship was tossed and torn,
Resistance was steadily falling,
A life with edges well worn.

Shelter was the desperate need
From the foolishness of sailing alone.
The power and danger of the sea
Caused the strong hunger for home.

The haven appeared just ahead
When hope had set like the sun.
The quiet place of protection,
The harbor of Psalm fifty-one.

"Have mercy," the sailor cried out,
"Tender mercies, that's what I need.
Cleanse me from all my iniquity
And each wicked and unclean deed.

"Purge me with Your Spirit,
Wash me and make me whole.
Make me hear joy and gladness
Within the depths of my soul.

"Create in me a clean heart
So I can teach others Your ways,
And drop anchor in this harbor
For all the rest of my days."

Grace

Have the wind and waves of sin
Driven you to the end of yourself,
And like David and many since
You long for spiritual health?

Come join with me in the safety
Of a place near God's own Son.
Finding grace and forgiveness
In the harbor of Psalm fifty-one.

*[1] To the chief Musician, A Psalm of David, when Nathan
the prophet came unto him, after he had gone in to
Bathsheba.*

*Have mercy upon me, O God, according to thy
lovingkindness: according unto the multitude of thy tender
mercies blot out my transgressions. [2] Wash me thoroughly
from mine iniquity, and cleanse me from my sin. [3] For I
acknowledge my transgressions: and my sin is ever before
me. [4] Against thee, thee only, have I sinned, and done this
evil in thy sight: that thou mightest be justified when thou
speakest, and be clear when thou judgest. [5] Behold, I was
shapen in iniquity, and in sin did my mother conceive me. [6]
Behold, thou desirest truth in the inward parts: and in the
hidden part thou shalt make me to know wisdom. [7] Purge
me with hyssop, and I shall be clean: wash me, and I shall
be whiter than snow. [8] Make me to hear joy and gladness;
that the bones which thou hast broken may rejoice. [9] Hide
thy face from my sins, and blot out all mine iniquities. [10]
Create in me a clean heart, O God; and renew a right spirit
within me. [11] Cast me not away from thy presence; and take
not thy holy spirit from me. [12] Restore unto me the joy of
thy salvation; and uphold me with thy free spirit. [13] Then
will I teach transgressors thy ways; and sinners shall be
converted unto thee.*

Psalm 51:1-13
A Psalm of Penitence

The Hand of Grace

When I see how the world around me has moved to lower standards in so many areas of life, I wonder how long God will withhold His judgment. Even in my life, as I recognize my sin, I am so grateful that God deals with me by reaching out a hand of mercy and grace. His hand is stretched out still to a lost and dying world and also to His children. We need to tell others about His hand of mercy and grace before it is too late and they must deal with His hand of judgment.

I reached out for my child one day
As we approached a busy street,
To protect him from traffic
And the danger we might meet.

Place your hand in mine, Son,
Stick close, right by my side.
You will be safe here with me,
Good judgment will be supplied.

My hand has moved to discipline
The errant ways of my son.
Correction is always unpleasant,
It is a task that must be done.

My hand is linked to the heart
As it protects the one I love,
While chastening wayward acts
That displease the Lord above.

This is a picture of God's love,
As He reaches to the human race
And touches each of our lives,
Reaching out with the hand of grace.

Grace

Many are in such great danger
While eternity lingers so near,
The message of the Savior's love
They desperately need to hear.

God wants to touch their hearts,
To cleanse them from every sin,
But they must open their being
And invite the Savior within.

His hand can deliver judgment,
Yet His arm is not too short to save,
And you can play a great part,
If true ministry you will crave.

Take news of His hand of grace
To those who have not known.
Touch their lives with your heart,
Until God's love is clearly shown.

We must demonstrate the message
That His hand is stretched out still.
God wants our hands to reach out,
The great commission to fulfill.

Behold, the LORD'S hand is not shortened, that it cannot save; neither his ear heavy, that it cannot hear:
Isaiah 59:1

Graceful Breezes

Imagine the freshness of a warm spring day, the sun kissing your skin and a gentle breeze caressing your face. It is an example of the graceful breezes of God that refresh us as we spend time with Him and His word.

Floating like a falling leaf
I find myself drifting in life,
On the gentle breath of God
Even when amid painful strife.

I consider the important role
God's graceful breezes play,
As they blow across my path
Caressing my heart every day.

The world sends great storms
To buffet my heart and soul.
Your quiet, heavenly breezes
Remind me of who's in control.

Graceful breezes can be found
Each time we open God's Word
And let His breath fall upon us
Causing our spirits to be stirred.

Yes, drifting away in my thoughts
Like a soaring bird on two wings,
Held aloft by graceful breezes
And lifted above earthly things.

There is a place of rest and peace
That quiet garden if you will,
Where the Spirit of God speaks
And all else is perfectly still.

Relax and enjoy sweet harmony
When more like Jesus you grow,
As you find that place of mercy
Where His graceful breezes blow.

The wind bloweth where it listeth, and thou hearest the sound thereof, but canst not tell whence it cometh, and whither it goeth: so is every one that is born of the Spirit.
John 3:8

Scenes of Life

The Lost Tooth
The Lantern
Storms Clouds
My Son
God Stood the Night Watch
Going Home
The Banquet
Special Love
A Parent's Prayer
First Day of School
A Letter from an Old Friend
The Newborn

The Lost Tooth

It is amazing to me how the little things can provide us with such wonderful memories and remind us of the spiritual things. Look for God's hand in every situation of life.

Suddenly loose and wiggly,
Reaching for her front tooth,
She was about to experience
A common passage of youth.

Soon the task was accomplished,
Leaving a gap she could not hide.
Opening a place of emergence,
For a new tooth deep down inside.

There was some initial fear,
Of what she did not understand.
But fear gave way to faith,
To trust in her daddy's hand.

With a little piece of string
Tied carefully round about,
He simply gave a quick pull—
Yanked that little tooth out.

The old makes way for the new
Just like in spiritual things.
Letting go of that which is past
And the regret that it brings.

Growing up into God's new plan,
The maturity that He desires.
Replacing the milk of the Word
With flaming spiritual fires.

The gaps created by surrender
Will soon be filled by His love.
With new tools for us to use
To further His Kingdom above.

Learning to trust God's hand
Like a child in her daddy's care,
Allows Him to lead and guide us
As our life with Him we share.

7 Ask, and it shall be given you; seek, and ye shall find;
knock, and it shall be opened unto you: 8 For every one that
asketh receiveth; and he that seeketh findeth; and to him
that knocketh it shall be opened. 9 Or what man is there of
you, whom if his son ask bread, will he give him a stone? 10
Or if he ask a fish, will he give him a serpent? 11 If ye then,
being evil, know how to give good gifts unto your children,
how much more shall your Father which is in heaven give
good things to them that ask him?
Matthew 7:7~11

The Lantern

When walking in the darkness there is always fear about what is up ahead. When walking with the Lord Jesus Christ we are never in the dark, and fear is not invited to tag along.

I remember long years ago
Visiting grandfather's farm.
I don't recall all the details
Except for the big red barn.

Out a ways from the house
Standing tall and very wide,
With many things of interest
Just waiting for me inside.

A great place for adventure
And my boyish explorations,
Providing quality material
For my vivid imaginations.

One night a storm blew in,
It woke us all with sound.
The wind was heavy and wet
And darkness was all around.

Grandpa headed for the barn,
An old lantern lit the way.
We waited for his return
Hoping everything was OK.

The time just seemed to crawl
And grandma wanted to check,
Wondering if all was well—
Her nerves were really a wreck.

She took my small hand in hers
And out the back door we went,
Down a dark but beaten path
Toward a memorable event.

On a night so dark, so stormy,
We felt our steps inch along,
Looking through the gate
For a clue to what was wrong.

Then we saw that old lantern
Up ahead of us once more,
Hanging all alone on a peg
Next to that great barn door.

Relieved we found grandpa
Tending to the stock inside,
Expecting us to follow, he left
A light the storm couldn't hide.

My childhood recollections
Were about the mystery of it all,
The late night expedition
That ended in a cattle stall.

Yet I am sometimes reminded
Of dark storms along our path,
As we live in times of crisis
A world of danger and wrath.

Jesus said, "I will be your light
Just like a lantern on a hill.
And in the midst of the storm
I'll help your heart be still."

So set your eyes on the Savior
In the midst of darkest night,
And through the storms of life
He will provide a living light.

Then spake Jesus again unto them, saying, I am the light of the world: he that followeth me shall not walk in darkness, but shall have the light of life.
John 8:12

Storm Clouds

Dealing with storm clouds and the difficulties they bring often causes us to lose our spiritual focus. We allow the howling wind to divert our attention from that still small voice that tells us, "I am the Master of the storm and the Creator of peace."

God has said of those that go
Down to the sea in great ships,
His wonders in the deep to see
Bringing praises to their lips.

How He commands elements
And raises the stormy wind,
Which lifts the watery waves
And sends them back again.

Our lives are like a vessel
Sailing upon restless seas,
Seeking our way in great waters,
Looking for a kindly breeze.

When on the horizon we see
Storm clouds blowing our way,
We must decide in whom we trust,
The One that winds must obey.

When the winds of adversity
Come rising on every side,
Where will I turn my craft
And where will my hope abide?

With sorrows rolling my way
Like billows on the ocean,
Will I hide in the shadow
Of His sacrificial devotion?

If we cry out to our Savior,
When trouble doth overwhelm,
His love calms our heart,
And His hand takes the helm.

He makes the storm to calm
And the waves thereof to still,
Bringing us the desired haven,
Finding peace within His will.

Oh lead me by Your goodness
For storms I don't understand,
Yet I know You are the answer,
And I am safe within Your hand.

22 And straightway Jesus constrained his disciples to get
into a ship, and to go before him unto the other side, while
he sent the multitudes away 23 And when he had sent the
multitudes away, he went up into a mountain apart to
pray: and when the evening was come, he was there alone. 24
But the ship was now in the midst of the sea, tossed with
waves: for the wind was contrary. 25 And in the fourth
watch of the night Jesus went unto them, walking on the
sea... 30 But when he saw the wind boisterous, he was afraid;
and beginning to sink, he cried, saying, Lord, save me. 31
And immediately Jesus stretched forth his hand, and
caught him, and said unto him, O thou of little faith,
wherefore didst thou doubt? 32 And when they were come
into the ship, the wind ceased. 33 Then they that were in the
ship came and worshipped him, saying, Of a truth thou art
the Son of God.
Matthew 14:22~33

My Son

This is an account of an incident that took place in the life of my pastor, Thomas R. Downs, and his parents. James 5:16 says..."The fervent prayer of a righteous man availeth much." In this case, a future servant of God was called back to a right relationship with his Lord. Should you be praying for someone like this young man, or are you like this young man and someone is praying for you? Either way, do what's right!

Troubled and broken in heart,
Over so many painful years,
Looking for missing pieces,
And the answer to bitter tears.

Oh, God, my son has wandered,
Living in the wilderness of sin.
His mother and I kneel tonight,
Not knowing where to begin.

We think of his days of youth,
Steps following after the Lord,
Sharing the truth with others,
Being grounded in the Word.

Now the times are different.
How quickly life has changed.
His decisions have faltered
And priorities rearranged.

Not walking in Your statutes
Nor living in Godly ways,
Surrendering to the flesh,
The world has filled his days.

Scenes of Life

We have prayed for his return
To the Lord who saved his soul,
And have asked for intervention
To make him spiritually whole.

Resistance has been his answer
To our heart-felt call and plea.
"I'll take care of living my life.
I am responsible, just me".

You have commanded us to come.
Yes, so boldly to Your throne
Bringing our every petition,
This heartache we have known.

We are ready to give him up
And to take this final stand.
We urge the heart of our Lord,
To move with a strong hand.

Bring him home dead or alive.
This is our fervent prayer:
Alive to Christ to serve Him,
Or into Your eternal care.

The sound of this fatal petition
Does cause our hearts to fear.
Yet the comforting Holy Spirit
Tenderly hovers so near.

In a car somewhere across town
Rebelling hands began to shake.
A son stared death in the face,
And knew a choice he must make.

Trembling, he drove back home,
Knocked on his parent's door,
Brokenness entered his heart—
"I can't live this way anymore."

"We just prayed and gave you up.
We didn't know you might come.
God has answered our hearts
And sent back our wayward son."

The war was not concluded
But the battle had been turned.
The flesh would not go easily,
Many bridges had to be burned.

The elderly saints had prayed,
Friends and family joined in.
The first steps of his journey
On that night they did begin.

The process of repentance
Starts deep within the heart
And invades our very being
As old patterns we depart.

Today our son is seeking
To walk in the Spirit each day,
Spending time in God's Word,
To keep him from drifting away.

New crossroads will appear
And God's grace will prevail.
As his failures he confesses,
God's mercy will never fail.

Thank you, Lord, for bringing
To pass that decisive night.
All the glory belongs to You.
Our son has done what's right.

*30 Therefore I will judge you, O house of Israel, every one
according to his ways, saith the Lord GOD. Repent, and
turn yourselves from all your transgressions; so iniquity
shall not be your ruin. 31 Cast away from you all your
transgressions, whereby ye have transgressed; and make
you a new heart and a new spirit: for why will ye die, O
house of Israel? 32 For I have no pleasure in the death of
him that dieth, saith the Lord GOD: wherefore turn
yourselves, and live ye.*
Ezekiel 18:30~32

God Stood the Night Watch

Written for the family of J. Thomas Downs and all those whose loved ones have struggled in their last days. God is ever-present in their situations and knows they can only do so much.

The hour, it was late,
I had done all I could.
The saint struggled on
As helpless I stood.

I knew the great promise
In my heart of hearts.
God always finishes
The good work He starts.

When the crossing comes
I desire to be there,
To stand with my dear one
This moment to share.

But God did not will it
To be as I would choose,
But His grace is sufficient
This I will not lose.

For when the time came
For this saint to go through,
God stood the night watch.
He will, for you, too.

4 *Sing unto the LORD, O ye saints of his, and give thanks at the remembrance of his holiness.* 5 *For his anger endureth but a moment; in his favour is life: weeping may endure for a night, but joy cometh in the morning.*
Psalm 30:4~5

Going Home

What a privilege to be present at the home going of one of God's saints. The blessed hope and comfort of knowing that you have surrendered your loved one into the arms of Jesus is indescribable. These things are never easy but neither was Calvary. Consider the great benefit to those who now live in the presence of Jesus.

A hush came over the family,
Their beloved lingered near,
That crossing over time
A call she soon would hear.

Weary was her condition.
How long could the fight go?
When would the Lord answer?
It seemed impossible to know.

There was a special presence
Sensed by some in the room.
Movement in a spiritual plane,
The feeling of hope, not doom.

The breathing was so labored,
And now it seemed too slow.
We agreed in prayer together,
It was time that we let her go.

Yet there was a bond so strong
That years had sewn in place,
The fabric of a family's love
Knit together by God's grace.

What a privilege to be there
When a saint of God goes home.
It seems the Savior beckoned
With open arms saying "Shalom."

My mind imagined within,
That He carried her as a babe
In His bosom so very close,
This one He had died to save.

She is gone and we hold hands.
Our tears hold joy and pain,
But hope wells within us,
In Christ we'll meet again.

We prayed, we thanked our God
That she had trusted in Him,
And blessed each of our lives
With her presence therein.

Precious in the sight of the LORD is the death of his saints.
Psalm 116:15

The Banquet

More times than we would care to admit our stomachs start to call when the pastor reaches the last point of his message and we begin to think about that Sunday meal. Or perhaps, you can remember that favorite meal that your mother or grandmother prepared for you. It makes us hungry just thinking about it. Jesus has prepared a heavenly feast for us and invites each of His children to come and dine with Him on a daily basis. If you have been missing this divine buffet, your life will quickly show the effects of spiritual malnutrition and begin to atrophy. Take hold of God's Word and meet Him for a daily dinner that will bless your life.

I've been invited to a banquet
With my Savior, Lord and King
All that's needed is provided,
I don't have to bring a thing.

When Jesus said, "Come and dine,"
I agreed to accept His call;
But some friends came with me
As I went to the dining hall.

When we sat down at His table,
My old pride pulled up a chair,
No invitation had been made
Yet vanity didn't seem to care.

Along with pride came my will,
I never thought he would show
And as others tried to enter,
I knew they would have to go.

Jesus rises from His seat
And with all authority attests,
"This banquet is just for two
So outside with all the rest.

"This is a private appointment,
Just between My child and Me.
When the two of us are together
There is no need to make it three.

"We are going to talk about life
And the steps along the way,
The need to follow directions
To accomplish My work each day."

There are some warnings needed
The great danger that is near,
And the power of the Spirit
That helps me not to fear.

Through each dinner course
I am nourished deep within,
His love so clearly displayed
As He cleanses me from sin.

What a privilege to partake of
This divine heavenly repast;
Yet when invited to come each day,
All too often I choose to fast.

Have you deserted this banquet,
A spiritual feast with the King,
Malnourished on the inside
And weakened in everything?

Think on the things of His word,
And develop a hunger down deep.
Dinner is served in the palace,
And you have an appointment to keep.

Jesus saith unto them, Come and dine. And none of the disciples durst ask him, Who art thou? knowing that it was the Lord.
John 21:12

Special Love

Do we have time and are we inclined to serve people who are in difficult situations? In our perceived strength, we sometimes forget how the Savior came to us in our greatest need and expects us to reach out to others in like manner.

God's immediate attention
Is called to events on earth,
As examples of special love
Display a heavenly worth.

When the hours of early morn
Find a mother with her child,
As the fever runs its course,
Her care so tender and mild.

A family opens its heart
To a child that is not theirs,
And raises him as their own
Making him one of the heirs.

A child cares for the parent
Whose body has begun to fail,
With the years taking a toll,
Leaving them so very frail.

A woman faces the last days
With he who shared her life,
Through the tears showing
The love of a faithful wife.

The couple on their knees
Pleading their son's case,
That God will bring him back
From a lifestyle so very base.

The witness with a message
Weeping for a poor lost soul,
Needing God's amazing grace
To become spiritually whole.

When we reach out to weak ones
With the heart as unto our Lord,
We serve those He called "least"
And strike a heavenly chord.

And the King shall answer and say unto them, Verily I say unto you, Inasmuch as ye have done it unto one of the least of these my brethren, ye have done it unto me.
Matthew 25:40

A Parent's Prayer

Written with thoughts of Kyle, Kevin, Greg, Libi and all children who face major childhood illnesses and disabilities. How God uses them to bless our lives with their love and remind us of how much we have to be thankful. Do you know of a family in these circumstances who need you to faithfully remember them in prayer?

Dear Lord, I need Your help
As You know my child is ill.
My heart is heavy within me
I come now seeking Your will.

You have given him to me
Showing Your grace so plain.
I know You want the best for us
Even when I witness his pain.

Oh, God, my child is so fearful
Of doctors and tests and such.
Though I desire to help him,
I find I am afraid just as much.

He tries to understand it all
And just why he must endure.
He looks to me for comfort
But I can't provide the cure.

You know all about suffering,
Watching Your Son on earth,
Bleeding and dying for our sin,
Providing for the new birth.

Give me strength in this crisis
As I stand by my ailing child,
To hold him while he is crying
With arms so loving and mild.

Please send to us each hour
A touch of Your special grace,
And help my son to trust You
In all the trials that we face.

Hold his hand, hold his heart,
This tender lamb so small.
Oh, lead us Gentle Shepherd,
And love us through it all.

*8 For this thing I besought the Lord thrice, that it might
depart from me. 9 And he said unto me, My grace is
sufficient for thee: for my strength is made perfect in
weakness. Most gladly therefore will I rather glory in my
infirmities, that the power of Christ may rest upon me. 10
Therefore I take pleasure in infirmities, in reproaches, in
necessities, in persecutions, in distresses for Christ's sake: for
when I am weak, then am I strong.*
II Corinthians 12:8-10

First Day of School

Do your remember that first day of school for your child? What a blessing it is to watch them grow in grace over the years. Take good notes so you can remember when the years have flown by.

As I look upon this little one,
Given by God's precious hand,
Beginning a new adventure,
New things to understand,

The very first day of school
A special, important event;
God bless my dear young child
As I ponder where years went.

Seems like only days before
The first cry came to my ears,
As I held the babe in my arms
Rejoicing in love with tears.

Changes have come so quickly,
Growth and maturing abound.
Different, yet still the same,
A joy to my life I have found.

Growth in grace and wisdom
Is desperately needed today.
Who can I get to assist me
In teaching the proper way?

God give my child a teacher
That knows Your very heart,
Who will love her little ones
And give them a Godly start.

Teaching the mind to learn,
And helping the eyes to read,
Showing the heart wisdom,
And the truth that we all need.

This first day was a long one.
My heart was so concerned.
My child has been to school.
I wonder what was learned?

Train up a child in the way he should go: and when he is old, he will not depart from it.
Proverbs 22:6

A Letter from an Old Friend

You have connections with many people throughout your life who all share a common trait. They all have needs of one sort or another and of varying degrees. Yet the greatest need a person has is for a personal relationship with God. Sharing your personal experience with the Lord, with as many of those connections as you possibly can, will bear fruit for all of eternity.

I wrote a letter to an old friend
Whom I hadn't seen for a long time.
Just to find out about her life
And share some details of mine.

I told her how God had changed me
From the person she used to know,
And shown me a new way of life,
When salvation He did bestow.

I waited some time for an answer
To the inquiry that had been sent,
But no word was forthcoming,
No reply, not the smallest hint.

Then one day a letter arrived,
Yes, a letter from an old friend.
One that was filled with details
From the beginning to the end.

She told me a story of grace—
How God had entered her soul,
And through His Son Jesus
Had made her spiritually whole.

What a thrill to read the pages
Telling me the rest of the story
Unfolded in the life of a friend
Bringing only God the glory.

Perhaps you have an old friend
Whom you haven't seen for a while,
And a word from you fitly spoken,
Would bring to his face a smile.

Tell him all about your new life,
Just what God has done for you,
And you may end up rejoicing
When He touches his life too.

A word fitly spoken is like apples of gold in pictures of silver.
Proverbs 25:11

The Newborn

Written from the testimony of Amos Humphries regarding the birth of his first son, Jonathan Clay Humphries. It is amazing how those little gifts from God can take ownership of our hearts so quickly.

Today life seemed to begin
Like a clock starting to run.
I witnessed a miraculous event,
The birth of my firstborn son.

The struggle had been intense,
My wife fought through pain
God blessed in all the details
Of the process He did ordain.

As tiny lungs filled with air,
His very first cry did amaze.
The volume was almost as great
As my prayerful, joyful praise.

They attended his physical needs
So I moved to stand by his side,
Bending over near to his face,
Grateful tears I could not hide.

As I spoke to him so gently,
His spirit began to subside.
He knew my voice distinctly
From the time he was inside.

His hand touched my finger
And grasped just a little part.
As he held on to his father,
He took possession of my heart.

God help me to hold on to You,
Like this child holding my hand,
And to listen to Your voice,
As it helps me to understand.

Lord teach me how to teach him
To daily walk by Your grace,
Till one day we stand together
Before our loving Savior's face.

5 For thou, O God, hast heard my vows: thou hast given me the heritage of those that fear thy name. 8 So will I sing praise unto thy name for ever, that I may daily perform my vows.
Psalm 61:5 and 8

Seasons of Growth

The Courtroom

Entrée

The Deal

Reaching Down

He Remembered Me

Treasure

This I Know

The Broken Wing

The Diamond Cutter

The Tapestry of Love

Being There

The Courtroom

When we stand before God our guilt is so clear, and His mercy is so dear. How humbling it is to think that Jesus knew the desperate condition of my soul and yet paid full price for me!

A scene unfolds before me
In the courtroom of the King.
My case is being presented
With charges now to bring.

The books are opened wide
All entries are scanned,
It is obvious in an instant
I have no place to stand.

How can I hope to escape?
What defense can I plead?
It soon becomes very clear.
It is mercy that I need.

Yet no grounds for mercy;
The price it must be paid
For sins that I've committed,
And choices that were made.

The righteousness of God
Demands the full price.
No partial reimbursement—
Only total sacrifice.

What's needed is a witness.
Yes, one who will testify
To speak on my behalf,
Or my soul will surely die.

The Savior steps forward
Holding something near.
He offers it on my behalf,
His precious blood so dear.

The courtroom is silent.
The Father starts to speak.
"This is my Son who paid it all,
The satisfaction that I seek.

"Not guilty is my verdict
You are fully justified,
As righteous as the Lamb
Who for your sin has died."

My spirit, it is humbled,
As I fall upon my face.
Thankful for His mercy
And truly saving grace.

13 And you, being dead in your sins and the uncircumcision of your flesh, hath he quickened together with him, having forgiven you all trespasses; 14 Blotting out the handwriting of ordinances that was against us, which was contrary to us, and took it out of the way, nailing it to his cross;
Colossians 2:13~14

Entrée

There are times in life when we feel like we are in jail. Decisions we have made have placed us into bondage to one thing or another. When Paul and Silas met with God at midnight, bands were loosed and prison doors opened. Is there a midnight meeting on your agenda?

There was a soul in prison
Confined for just cause,
Sentenced and condemned
For violations of God's laws.

No hope of commutation,
The verdict just and fair,
Conditions cold and lonely,
Resigned to living there.

Then came the great news!
A call had come from the King,
Arrangements had been made,
New hope began to spring.

Unprepared was he to stand
In the presence of this One.
His clothing filthy rags
And appearance all undone.

Then came a special offer
From the King's only Son.
"Take My robe upon you,
It will cover all you've done."

Now the doors are opened
The Great One bids him come.
"My Son has paid for your sins,
All of them, not just some.

"Be seated here at My table.
By law you are now a son,
Adopted into the family,
Forever we will be as one."

His love now surrounds him.
He has forgotten prison fears.
But he remembers the day
God wiped away all his tears.

[25] And at midnight Paul and Silas prayed, and sang praises unto God: and the prisoners heard them. [26] And suddenly there was a great earthquake, so that the foundations of the prison were shaken: and immediately all the doors were opened, and every one's bands were loosed. [27] And the keeper of the prison awaking out of his sleep, and seeing the prison doors open, he drew out his sword, and would have killed himself, supposing that the prisoners had been fled. [28] But Paul cried with a loud voice, saying, Do thyself no harm: for we are all here. [29] Then he called for a light, and sprang in, and came trembling, and fell down before Paul and Silas, [30] And brought them out, and said, Sirs, what must I do to be saved? [31] And they said, Believe on the Lord Jesus Christ, and thou shalt be saved, and thy house.
Acts 16:25-31

The Deal

The Deal was written after the salvation of our church attorney on an evening when a major financial agreement was completed. Church leadership had prayed as each phase of the plan fell together and each time asked God to save the soul of our lawyer. At one point, he came into the room from negotiating with another party when we were just mentioning his name in prayer. He was used by God to help us greatly that night and just one hour later made an eternal deal of his own. God answered our prayer in a dramatic way that night.

Negotiations had started.
The terms were very clear.
I knew that I needed help.
Decision time was near.

My bargaining was weak.
All I had was my sin,
And as long as it was there
He would not let me in.

What manner of a deal
Gives everything for me?
A Savior that gave His life
As He hung upon the tree.

He asks only for a trade—
My sin, for mercy and grace.
He washes me with His blood.
I am clean without a trace.

Yes, we have an agreement,
That mistakes can never kill.
Between separated parties,
A great merger if you will.

Now I am in His family.
His presence is so real
Since I accepted His offer
And made the greatest deal.

[4] And my speech and my preaching was not with enticing words of man's wisdom, but in demonstration of the Spirit and of power: [5] That your faith should not stand in the wisdom of men, but in the power of God.
I Corinthians 2:4~5.

Reaching Down

Sometimes I wonder just how long the arm of God really is. Long enough to reach me is the answer that comes. What manner of God is He that He would die for my sin, for me, and then reach down into my heart and save me? I'll spend eternity learning the answer to that question.

An old friend used to sing
A song about the Savior's hand
Reaching down to rescue us
From a place of sinking sand.

He said my soul was lost
And my life all undone,
That I didn't know God's love,
And I didn't know His Son.

I remember many years ago
That day I saw the truth.
Yes, I was a big-time sinner,
Even though just a youth.

My friend sang so clearly
About our desperate need.
Lives all undone and ruined,
Yes, that was me indeed.

Way, way down God reached
To find this one in despair
And give me a brand new life
And a story of mercy to share.

Is your life filled with sin
And your heart all alone?
Have you started to reap
Wicked seeds you have sown?

The Savior died to save you
From a life that's all undone
And the sadness of living
Apart from God and His Son.

He is reaching down today
For sinners wandering afar.
Seek Him! He will save you
No matter where you are.

[1] To the chief Musician, A Psalm of David. I waited patiently for the LORD; and he inclined unto me, and heard my cry. [2] He brought me up also out of an horrible pit, out of the miry clay, and set my feet upon a rock, and established my goings. [3] And he hath put a new song in my mouth, even praise unto our God: many shall see it, and fear, and shall trust in the LORD.
Psalm 40:1~3

~In memory of A.T. Humphries~

He Remembered Me

Does God know you personally through His Son Jesus Christ? You can be sure He will never forget the name of one of His children. Just call out to Him in prayer. He will know who you are.

A great man came to town one day.
We had met just once before,
Being briefly introduced
While we stood by an open door.

It was only a fleeting moment
At the start of his rise to fame.
I was shocked as we spoke again.
You see, he remembered my name.

I don't pretend to importance,
Just your average kind of guy.
That he should have noticed me,
I have always wondered why.

This brings my thoughts to God,
His power and glory supreme.
He doesn't need to think of me,
Or so to my heart it would seem.

Yet before I was even born,
He knew all my details you see.
Who am I compared to a holy God
That He should remember me?

For years I didn't really know Him
Or consider His call on my life.
Then we met again through His Son,
Who rescued me from sin and strife.

My Savior brought me to His Father
And He remembered my name.
"I've got it written in the book,
And I'm extremely glad you came".

The Creator of this universe
Has graven my name on His hand.
He knows me, as His own child.
On this wonderful truth I stand.

Now if you want to know God,
You must seek Him through His Son.
When it comes to introductions,
Only Jesus can get it done.

He will present you faultless
With a heart whiter than snow,
And as a member of the family,
All heaven your name will know.

39 And one of the malefactors which were hanged railed on
him, saying, If thou be Christ, save thyself and us. 40 But
the other answering rebuked him, saying, Dost not thou
fear God, seeing thou art in the same condemnation? 41 And
we indeed justly; for we receive the due reward of our deeds:
but this man hath done nothing amiss. 42 And he said unto
Jesus, Lord, remember me when thou comest into thy
kingdom. 43 And Jesus said unto him, Verily I say unto
thee, To day shalt thou be with me in paradise.
Luke 23:39-43

Treasure

Placing a proper value on things is often an extremely difficult task for the buyer as well as the seller. The authenticity of the article bears great weight as to its ultimate value. In getting treasure, don't forget to lay hold of that which lasts forever, and whose value is beyond measure.

There are men of great riches,
Earthly treasures untold—
Things that sparkle in light
Possessions of purest gold.

They speak and many listen.
When they act others take note.
Looking to gain an advantage,
Their words they love to quote.

There are so many things to own.
Their eyes see a lot to desire.
Much of their time is spent
Seeing what they can acquire.

Worldly treasure has beauty.
Riches can give cause to sing,
Yet their usefulness to man
Is such a temporary thing.

But, oh, depth of the riches
Of our God in heaven above,
That has shown itself to us
In the form of Calvary's love.

How unsearchable to our minds
Are the judgments of the Lord.
He gave to us salvation
That no rich man could afford.

Wisdom so wonderfully vast
And His ways past finding out,
Knowledge beyond our capacity,
That we only can wonder about.

Seek Him and you will be rich.
Find Him and you will have peace.
Know Him and you will have life,
And treasure that never will cease.

1 Paul, an apostle of Jesus Christ by the will of God, to the
saints which are at Ephesus, and to the faithful in Christ
Jesus: 2 Grace be to you, and peace, from God our Father,
and from the Lord Jesus Christ. 3 Blessed be the God and
Father of our Lord Jesus Christ, who hath blessed us with
all spiritual blessings in heavenly places in Christ: 4 Ac-
cording as he hath chosen us in him before the foundation
of the world, that we should be holy and without blame
before him in love: 5 Having predestinated us unto the
adoption of children by Jesus Christ to himself, according to
the good pleasure of his will, 6 To the praise of the glory of
his grace, wherein he hath made us accepted in the beloved.
7 In whom we have redemption through his blood, the
forgiveness of sins, according to the riches of his grace; 8
Wherein he hath abounded toward us in all wisdom and
prudence;
Ephesians 1:1-8

This I Know

Have you ever met someone who gave you the impression that they thought that they knew everything? In this day and age of increased knowledge, it is impossible to know everything about any one given subject. What a blessing it is to be able to know some things for sure and beyond a shadow of a doubt! When you know the Savior personally, you don't know everything, but you know the One who does.

Some things I'm not sure about,
But some things I truly know.
Other things I'm just learning,
And my knowledge needs to grow.

I know that Jesus loves me,
His precious blood for me was shed,
And He wore the thorns of my sin,
Upon His innocent head.

I'm not sure just why He chose me,
Of all sinners I think I am chief,
And my heart above all others
Was in most need of relief.

I know that life is temporary,
That each day needs to count.
Yet ill spent and wasted time
Seems to continuously mount.

I'm not sure about tomorrow,
The things that may come to pass,
And the trials and temptations
He has told me will not last.

I know He is walking with me
Through each and every day.
He will never leave or forsake
And will keep me all the way.

I'm not sure just how to serve Him
For in my flesh I so often say no
To the leading of the Holy Spirit
When He prompts me to speak or go.

I know He is returning for me,
And eternity will be my home.
Then from His daily presence
This heart will never roam.

I'm not sure about your heart.
Have you invited God to abide
Within every facet of your life
And way down deep inside?

Some things I know for certain.
God's word has made them clear.
The rest will just have to wait,
Until the Savior's voice I hear.

For the which cause I also suffer these things: nevertheless I am not ashamed: for I know whom I have believed, and am persuaded that he is able to keep that which I have committed unto him against that day.
II Timothy 1:12

The Broken Wing

Our Savior is the answer for those with a broken life. Call on His name and He will provide all that you will ever need to fly and soar like an eagle.

There once was a little bird
Whose heart refused to sing,
Because there was a loss of hope—
She had suffered a broken wing.

Gone was the ability to soar
Above all the things of earth,
Trapped in hostile dimension
Wondering what life was worth.

Such a great lack of fulfillment—
Who needs a bird that can't fly,
Or do what she was born to do?
Might as well lie down and die.

Many, spiritually speaking,
Have lost their ability to fly.
Grounded like wounded eagles
Afraid to even step out and try.

Flying is such a simple task
For those equipped and strong
Who ride on heavenly breezes
And let the Lord give a song.

Are you one with this problem
No victory in spiritual things,
Wanting to take to the skies
But limited by broken wings?

Bring your life to the Master
He will make your heart to sing,
He specializes in healing hearts
And repairing a broken wing.

The spirit of the Lord GOD is upon me; because the LORD hath anointed me to preach good tidings unto the meek; he hath sent me to bind up the brokenhearted, to proclaim liberty to the captives, and the opening of the prison to them that are bound;
Isaiah 61:1

The Diamond Cutter

If you desire to reflect the light of God's love to those around you, the diamond cutter's work must be performed. When the facets of your life are properly shaped, light will emerge like laser beams on a dark night.

He considers the odd stone
With a sharply trained eye
And sees the value within.
His heart is moved to buy.

The great inward potential
To be a stone of great price
Will require special skill,
Hands that are so precise.

This diamond in the rough
Must be studied on each side
With a plan to remove defects
And flaws that tend to hide.

The chisel is put in place,
The hammer strikes a blow.
As pieces splinter and fall
The light begins to glow.

The craftsman slowly shapes
This masterpiece yet to be.
The sparkle of a finished work
His eyes are the first to see.

Light reflected abundantly
From each facet and its core,
With beauty we all can enjoy
Yet its meaning so much more.

Your heart is that diamond
In need of the Master's hand,
To help it reflect His love
To all who don't understand.

This process of refinement,
Chipping and cutting away,
Is never really that pleasant
And requires a desire to obey.

How wonderful is the result
When God shapes your heart
And removes the impurities,
Yes, those from the very start.

You can shine just like a gem
When the light of Christ is shown
Through a diamond in the rough
That became God's treasure stone.

14 Ye are the light of the world. A city that is set on an hill cannot be hid. 15 Neither do men light a candle, and put it under a bushel, but on a candlestick; and it giveth light unto all that are in the house. 16 Let your light so shine before men, that they may see your good works, and glorify your Father which is in heaven.

Matthew 5:14~16

The Tapestry of Love

Oh God, create a picture in my life of Your love and grace. Make it a tapestry that shows Your hand at work and brings glory and honor to Your Son Jesus Christ.

Studying beautiful patterns
And the artistry that I see,
Analyzing wonderful fabric
From a graceful tapestry.
The artist's internal vision
Unfolds as he moves his hand,
Colors delicately blended
And woven, strand by strand.
God desires to build your life
Like a great tapestry of love,
Designed by His divine will
From heavenly plans above.
Each phase of this living print
Develops in joys and trials,
As character is slowly formed
Midst many tears and smiles.
When the fabric of our life is
Pierced by needle and thread,
The image of the Savior
Within the tapestry is wed.
Allow the Master designer
To work His loving will in you,
And guide the development
Of your life and all you do.
The wonderful divine artwork
Which was begun at Calvary,
In God's gallery displayed
Throughout all eternity.

[20] But in a great house there are not only vessels of gold and of silver, but also of wood and of earth; and some to honour, and some to dishonour. [21] If a man therefore purge himself from these, he shall be a vessel unto honour, sanctified, and meet for the master's use, and prepared unto every good work.
II Timothy 2:20~21

Being There

Written immediately following an opportunity to pray with someone as they invited Jesus Christ to be their personal Lord and Savior.

There is not an event in this life
That can ever possibly compare
To witnessing the birth of a saint
From an intimate front row chair.

To see the drama of repentance
Unfolding before prayerful eyes,
As you witness a poor lost sinner
Making unbreakable spiritual ties.

Reaching up with sin-stained hands
Forgiveness so willingly is sought.
Reaching down with nail-scarred hands
Jesus claims the soul He has bought.

The heart of this quiet witness,
Repenting of its own private sin,
Prays for the next opportunity,
A new birth to witness yet again.

5 They that sow in tears shall reap in joy. 6 He that goeth forth and weepeth, bearing precious seed, shall doubtless come again with rejoicing, bringing his sheaves with him.
Psalm 126:5-6

Bible Scenes

In Chambers

The Soldier

The Promise

Shut in by Grace

To Dream Again

The Plague

The Fool

The Struggle

This Is My Battle

In Chambers

The issue is not whether you or I have sinned, for we all have and will again sin. The crux is, when confronted by the Spirit of God regarding our sin, will we confess it and repent.

A King entered his chambers
The charges were on his mind,
Spoken by the prophet Nathan
Naming sin of the worst kind.

The shame was overwhelming
Guilt was crushing his soul,
Was there even a possibility
That he could ever be whole?

Down on his face before God
Shaken and broken within,
Never intending this evil
The harm that it would begin.

Guilty—yes, so very guilty.
My life is Yours to read.
Blot out my transgressions.
Send the mercy that I need.

Teach me, Lord, who You are,
One who can cleanse the heart
And take a man who has failed
Giving him a brand new start.

The voice of the great I Am
Says, "I forgive. It is now done.
All your sins are blotted out,
Covered by the blood of My Son."

The King rises from the floor.
The color returns to his face.
He purposes to serve his God,
An example of heavenly grace.

A man after Gods own heart
Because he knew how to repent,
Thanking God for the freedom
And the messenger He had sent.

*5 And David's anger was greatly kindled against the man;
and he said to Nathan, As the LORD liveth, the man that
hath done this thing shall surely die: 6 And he shall restore
the lamb fourfold, because he did this thing, and because he
had no pity.7 and Nathan said to David, Thou art the
man ...and David said unto Nathan, I have sinned
against the Lord.*
II Samuel 12:1~13

The Soldier

Can we stand for that which is right in the face of violent adversity? God says you can, and if you do, He will personally take note. If we are willing to live a sold out life for our Lord, dying for Him will not be a problem.

A humbleness of spirit comes,
Looking back across the years
At a life given for our Lord,
Its impact never disappears.

A man full of faith and power
Touching lives at every hand,
Willing to serve his Savior
And take an eternal stand.

Stephen was just such a man.
Apostle's hands on him were laid.
Only his heavenly Father knew
The great price that would be paid.

Men with religious renown,
They disputed as he testified.
His life filled with the Spirit—
Wisdom that could not be denied.

They brought him to the council
And said he had blasphemed,
Yet as he stood before them
His joyful face just beamed.

He answered from the Scripture
Many things that they had heard,
About the promises of God,
The blessing that had occurred.

He said that they never listened
And the prophets they persecuted.
Then when God sent His own Son
His teachings they disputed.

Stiff-necked and hard of heart
With ears that will not hear,
"You killed your own Messiah
And you have much to fear."

They could not stand his words
Their hearts were deeply cut.
Though he had the truth of heaven
His mouth they sought to shut.

"I see God's throne in heaven,"
Stephen said above the clatter,
"And the Savior standing there.
That's all that seems to matter."

Soon the events raged onward
He was stoned outside the gate,
Asking God to forgive them,
Showing compassion so great.

Yes, Jesus was not seated,
But standing at the throne,
Attentive to that great scene
To welcome His soldier home.

This crowd was encouraged
By a young man named Saul,
Who fought against the church
But soon would hear God's call.

He would take up the message
That Stephen had died to give
And share it with the world
For as long as he should live.

The Savior waits to receive
Soldiers who will live for Him,
And when their work is finished
He will rise to welcome them.

And he kneeled down, and cried with a loud voice, Lord, lay not this sin to their charge. And when he had said this, he fell asleep.
Acts 7:1~60

The Promise

God has invited us to join His family and sit at His table. This relationship is offered through the sacrifice of His Son on Calvary. He invites us to come as this young man, offering nothing but a desire to receive the favor of the King.

He was a child of royalty,
But had been crippled by a fall.
A story not unlike our position,
The damage sin caused in us all.

But a promise had been given
By someone who would be king,
"Don't worry about your family.
I'll take care of everything."

Years passed and events unfolded,
David finally sat on the throne.
He remembered his promise,
Yet the boy he had not known.

He lived in a place called barren,
Kept hidden by a faithful few
And wondered about his life.
There wasn't much he could do.

David had known this boy's father,
Dear friends were Jonathan and he,
Like two keys played on a piano
That together made harmony.

A servant advised the king
Where this boy did reside.
"Invite him to come to my palace
My love I will not hide."

Soon this one arrives
And comes before the king,
"I am just a broken vessel
And can't offer you anything."

"You shall sit at my table
As if you were my only son.
Past problems are all covered
A brand new life has begun."

What a wonderful picture
Is here so clearly shown,
Of God's amazing grace.
Yes, we know we are never alone.

We often limp when we walk
Because of the effect of sin.
In Christ all is forgiven
He helps us start over again.

We are adopted into His family.
He sought us where we were,
Invited us to eat at His table
And enjoy His love so pure.

His promise is not forgotten—
To rescue this fallen race
And provide for us a Savior
Who would suffer in our place.

He now calls you to His side.
Bring Him all your crippling sin,
And enjoy His wonderful peace
As His family you enter in.

Thank you Lord for this story
Of a crippled boy and a king.
A relationship we can possess
When to Jesus our heart we bring.

Broken and offering nothing
But a life of feeling alone,
In Christ made worthy to stand
Before God's heavenly throne.

*1 And David said, Is there yet any that is left of the house
of Saul, that I may show him kindness for Jonathan's sake?
9 Then the king called to Ziba, Saul's servant, and said
unto him, I have given unto thy master's son all that
pertained to Saul and to all his house. 10 Thou therefore,
and thy sons, and thy servants, shall till the land for him,
and thou shalt bring in the fruits, that thy master's son
may have food to eat: but Mephibosheth thy master's son
shall eat bread alway at my table. Now Ziba had fifteen
sons and twenty servants. 11 Then said Ziba unto the king,
According to all that my lord the king hath commanded his
servant, so shall thy servant do. As for Mephibosheth, said
the king, he shall eat at my table, as one of the king's sons.
12 And Mephibosheth had a young son, whose name was
Micha. And all that dwelt in the house of Ziba were
servants unto Mephibosheth. 13 So Mephibosheth dwelt in
Jerusalem: for he did eat continually at the king's table;
and was lame on both his feet.*

II Samuel 9:1~13

Shut in by Grace

Being closed inside of God's protection is a benefit of being found "in Christ Jesus." By His Grace we get in and by His Grace we stay in. That means He provides for all the details, and we just go along for the ride.

Wickedness on every hand
As mankind did his best
To try every evil thing
And put God to the test.

In looking for someone
With righteousness inside,
A spiritual remnant,
For His mercy to reside.

He found a faithful man,
Gave him a difficult task.
He responded obediently
And did all God would ask.

He built a large vessel.
God provided the prints.
His family was there to serve
And give some helpful hints.

When God had seen enough
Of mankind's revolting sin,
He sent Noah the animals
And told them to enter in.

With his family by his side
And the animals in place,
God closed the great door
And shut them in by grace.

Judgment fell from above
Thus mankind met its fate
Ignoring God's warnings,
And now it was too late.

There is a coming judgment
That will take you like a flood
Unless you place your life
Under Christ's shed blood.

It's called a place of mercy
Provided by God's own Son,
Within that ark of safety,
Shut in and forever done.

Jesus Christ is the only door,
Your chance to get on board.
Come in to eternal refuge,
All Heaven is your reward.

*13 In the selfsame day entered Noah, and Shem, and Ham,
and Japheth, the sons of Noah, and Noah's wife, and the
three wives of his sons with them, into the ark; 14 They, and
every beast after his kind, and all the cattle after their
kind, and every creeping thing that creepeth upon the earth
after his kind, and every fowl after his kind, every bird of
every sort 15 And they went in unto Noah into the ark, two
and two of all flesh, wherein is the breath of life. 16 And
they that went in, went in male and female of all flesh, as
God had commanded him: and the LORD shut him in.*
Genesis 7:13-16

To Dream Again

Do you remember the special times you have had with the Lord, like the day that you trusted Him as your personal Savior? How about the day He answered your prayer about the salvation of a friend or family member? Perhaps there was a special time when you totally surrendered your life to walk with the Lord. You shouldn't have to search very far back in your memory for those precious moments. God longs to give them to you on a regular basis. Don't let the circumstances and disappointments of life, take away your dream of living daily in obedient communion with Jesus Christ.

Some women went to the tomb,
To tend the body of their Lord,
A part of the ritual of death,
With spices they could afford.

God took note of their tears
And the deep personal sorrow,
The loss of the One they loved
With little hope for tomorrow.

What a wonderful dream it had been,
As He walked with them by the sea,
Telling them of the Father's love
And of His kingdom yet to be.

Now everything was different
And the dream seemed to be lost,
The grand purpose redemption,
But, oh, what a terrible cost!

As they examined the open tomb
An angel appeared and said,
"Why seek ye the living Savior,
Here in a place for the dead?"

"Alive!" they screamed and shouted,
When the others they did see.
"He is alive!" proclaimed another,
"He talked directly with me."

As these events began to unfold,
The Lord made His presence known,
Then very quickly left this earth,
To sit on His Father's throne.

They began to dream once more,
For He said He was coming again
To redeem the sons of Adam
From the very presence of sin.

Have you lost your heart's dream
Because of the entrance of sin?
Has a direction change occurred
In your goal of walking with Him?

Gather up that which is broken,
And bring all the pieces to Him.
Take hold of forgiving grace.
It's now time to dream again.

*3 And they entered in, and found not the body of the Lord
Jesus. 4 And it came to pass, as they were much perplexed
thereabout, behold, two men stood by them in shining
garments: 5 And as they were afraid, and bowed down their
faces to the earth, they said unto them, Why seek ye the
living among the dead? 6 He is not here, but is risen:
remember how he spake unto you when he was yet in
Galilee,*

Luke 24:3-6

The Plague

There are times in the life of believers when sin seems to be a plague that is out of control. Prayer, repentance, and resolutions only bring temporary relief. You must come to a place of true brokenness before the Savior, believing He will heal your heart. Purpose to enter Gods presence on a daily basis through His word. Find a godly friend, confess your battle to them, and enlist their help in holding you accountable to your spiritual commitment.

Moving through a crowd one day
Something very strange occurred.
While Jesus was healing others
The cry of a heart was heard.

The one who had been affected
Realized what He could do,
Believed if she could touch Him
She would receive a healing, too.

Reaching out to Him in faith,
Touching only a part of His coat,
As the plague of years fell away,
Jesus turned and took special note.

"Someone touched My clothes,"
Jesus asserted to those around.
Some said it was just the crowd,
The excitement, and the sound.

"No, this was the touch of faith
From one who was at wits end
And received what she had sought
When her affliction I did mend."

Stepping forth from the crowd,
She told Him she was the one.
He praised her simple faith to all
As a new found life was begun.

Has your strength finally failed in
Your battle with the plague of sin?
Do you long for sweet relief from
The defeat buried deep within?

Reach out and touch the Savior
Having faith in what He can do,
Offer Him the sins of a lifetime,
His gentle touch will heal you, too.

[27] When she had heard of Jesus, came in the press behind, and touched his garment. [28] For she said, If I may touch but his clothes, I shall be whole. [34] And he said unto her, Daughter, thy faith hath made thee whole; go in peace, and be whole of thy plague.
Mark 5:24-34

The Fool

When God speaks about the fool in Scripture we need to listen carefully because at times we act that way. If in practicality we ignore His presence, we take on the mantle of a fool.

The foolish man he hath said
Down in the depths of his heart,
"I think I know there is no God."
This is where he starts to depart.

For God has planted a seed
Within the heart of each man,
A message of His presence,
A brief outline of His plan.

Because they knew the truth
But chose to use their tools
To create their own little gods,
They earned the title of fools.

Thinking their way is right,
Not seeking to know His name,
Running after vile affections,
Finding in the end only shame.

While making a mockery of sin
They fill themselves with words.
And end up in the foolishness
Of worshipping beasts and birds.

Oh foolish man, please listen.
It is God, who holds the key
To the life filled with sin,
To making blinded eyes see.

Let Him rescue your heart
From a life of foolish things,
From the bondage of your error
And the darkness that it brings.

Open your life to His touch,
Ask Him to empower your eyes,
Then He will give you new life—
No longer the fool, but wise.

1 To the chief Musician, A Psalm of David. The fool hath said in his heart, There is no God. They are corrupt, they have done abominable works, there is none that doeth good.
2 The LORD looked down from heaven upon the children of men, to see if there were any that did understand, and seek God. 3 They are all gone aside, they are all together become filthy: there is none that doeth good, no, not one.
Psalm 14:1-3

The Struggle

Sitting in the bleachers, watching others play the game, is often entertaining but vicarious at best. God desires us to enter the arena and join in the battle with the flesh. Be sure to take your Elder Brother with you, He wins every time.

There is a battle raging
That confronts me every day,
A war within my members
Pulling me every which way.

In my spirit I know the truth
And agree to what is right.
In my flesh no quarter given,
Everything becomes a fight.

Oh, Lord, so often weariness
Brings me down to my knees.
I feel like a sin tossed ship,
Out on life's stormy seas.

You have invited me to come
With all the burdens I bear,
Offering sweet peace and rest
And all my loads to share.

Letting You confront my heart
When the things that I do
Are those I know are wrong
And so very offensive to You.

Yet, often I am a spectator
Watching others in the ring,
Dealing with You every day
Yielding gladly everything.

Paul said, "Who will deliver
Me from the struggle I fight,
Within this body of flesh
And help me do what's right?"

Jesus Christ was his answer,
And He is my answer today.
To have victory in the battle
He must lead me all the way.

23 But I see another law in my members, warring against
the law of my mind, and bringing me into captivity to the
law of sin which is in my members. 24 O wretched man that
I am! Who shall deliver me from the body of this death? 25 I
thank God through Jesus Christ our Lord. So then with the
mind I myself serve the law of God; but with the flesh the
law of sin.
Romans 7:23~25

THIS IS MY BATTLE

We often desire to intervene in a situation with our own skills and ideas, when God really wants to show Himself mighty in the solution of the problem. This does not mean that we are to always sit back and ignore responsibilities we know are ours, but if the battle is truly His, then there are times when we need to get out of the way and let Him work. If you allow the Spirit to lead you, He will clearly show you the things He wants you to handle.

"Child, this is My battle,"
Came the Word of the Lord
Standing before him,
In His hand the sword.

"This struggle is Mine
Your strength won't do
Rest in My provision
I will win it for you.

"The enemy is powerful.
His strongholds are high.
In warfare his minions
Have never been shy.

"My strength is perfected
When weakness you claim,
Going as your Champion
When you call My name."

Yes, this battle, it is His.
The victory has been won.
Lift voices now in praise
Of wonders God has done.

13 *And it came to pass, when Joshua was by Jericho, that he*
lifted up his eyes and looked, and, behold, there stood a man
over against him with his sword drawn in his hand: and
Joshua went unto him, and said unto him, Art thou for us,
or for our adversaries? 14 *And he said, Nay; but as captain*
of the host of the LORD am I now come. And Joshua fell
on his face to the earth, and did worship, and said unto
him, What saith my lord unto his servant? 15 *And the*
captain of the LORD'S host said unto Joshua, Loose thy
shoe from off thy foot; for the place whereon thou standest
is holy. And Joshua did so.
Joshua 5:13~15

Toward Home

Walking Confession's Road

Crossroads

Directions

Come Home

Walking Home

The Gathering

Suppertime

Standing at the Door

Behold the Lamb

Walking Confession's Road

There is something about confessing sin that my flesh hates. I seem to always pile up a great heap before I get around to dealing with God. Walking confession's road is a daily experience that keeps our sin account a short one.

There is a path to be traveled,
That starts at Calvary's hill.
We find judicial forgiveness
Where the Savior's blood did spill.

Sins are covered for eternity.
We are free from our guilty load.
Our heavenly Father now asks us
To start living by His new code.

The daily recognition of sin,
The foolishness we have sowed,
Can be dealt with by mercy
When walking confession's road.

We must see every one of our sins
As if looking thru God's own eye,
Instead of comparison to others
So we can carelessly justify.

Adopted is our new position,
In God's family placed as a child,
Needing parental forgiveness
For choices that have defiled.

Oft times the road from Calvary
Does twists and turns contain.
Our focus must be on the Savior.
His love it will constrain.

Some sit by the side of the road
Stuck in the cares of this world,
Waiting for a call to come home,
God's banner not quite unfurled.

Great joy comes with cleansing,
Spiritual washing of our feet,
Admitting each day every sin,
Even those which we repeat.

Don't leave this Godly route,
Make repentance your abode.
You will find God's joy in full,
As you walk confession's road.

*8 If we say that we have no sin, we deceive ourselves, and the
truth is not in us. 9 If we confess our sins, he is faithful and
just to forgive us our sins, and to cleanse us from all
unrighteousness. 10 If we say that we have not sinned, we
make him a liar, and his word is not in us.*
I John 1:8-10

Crossroads

As God brings you to a crossroad of decision, your will is exposed, and the picture is often not a pretty one. Each crossroad has a cross to be borne or ignored with the consequences that follow.

In traveling through a lifetime
One comes to a place of choice,
Whether to turn here or there
On advice from a whispered voice.

The choosing of a direction
From among the compass points,
Oft times a tremendous effort,
Brings pain to bones and joints.

Where to turn from here, Lord.
I know You are leading the way.
Why is it that I fail to listen?
Why is it Lord, I just cannot say.

The enticement of the moment
Selfishness You cannot abide,
The fear of what You require
When You ask me to turn aside.

My heart, it pounds within me
When You call and ask for more.
You lead me down a hallway
And toward a yet locked door.

The wooing of the Holy Spirit
Helps me to again realize
The truth so clearly visible
To willingly blinded eyes.

Each crossroads we encounter
Can never be counted as a loss
Providing that we remember,
Each crossroad has a cross.

Our headstrong will is taken
And is nailed upon the tree,
Each time we choose surrender
To become what He wants us to be.

15 *And if it seem evil unto you to serve the LORD, choose*
you this day whom ye will serve; whether the gods which
your fathers served that were on the other side of the flood,
or the gods of the Amorites, in whose land ye dwell: but as
for me and my house, we will serve the LORD. 16 *And the*
people answered and said, God forbid that we should forsake
the LORD, to serve other gods; 17 *For the LORD our God,*
he it is that brought us up and our fathers out of the land
of Egypt, from the house of bondage, and which did those
great signs in our sight, and preserved us in all the way
wherein we went, and among all the people through whom
we passed: 18 *And the LORD drave out from before us all*
the people, even the Amorites which dwelt in the land:
therefore will we also serve the LORD; for he is our God.
Joshua 24:15-18

Directions

The decision that faces us all is not what we will do, but whose will is to be followed. When we surrender in obedience to the leading of the Holy Spirit, the choices in our life became clear.

Looking back on things of the past
We see the wonders You have done.
You took strangers into Your fold
And knit them together as one.

The blessings You have bestowed,
The mercies that flow like the tide,
Have created in us a new heart
And changed us deep down inside.

Looking forward we stand in awe
At what You could help us to be.
The souls that hang in the balance,
Lord help us that we might see.

The crossroad of spiritual decision
Requires the surrender of the will.
Like You demonstrated in pattern
As You climbed up Calvary's hill.

Looking up we give You praise,
For whither, Lord, could we go?
Who else has the words of life
Whose love we can deeply know?

The time, it appears to be short.
Lord teach us to number our days
That when we stand before You
Many new ones will join us in praise

5 Trust in the LORD with all thine heart; and lean not unto thine own understanding. 6 In all thy ways acknowledge him, and he shall direct thy paths.
Proverbs 3:5&6

Come Home

God's call to us is usually in the form of one word—Come. Bring your fears, problems, dreams, failures, your whatever, and "Come unto me."

Today I feel so incredibly small—
Sin has again found an abiding place.
" Come home," says the all-loving Father.
"Let us carefully consider your case."

Dishonoring His investment in me,
A charge that is clearly deserved,
I oft wonder would it not be better
That my standing not be preserved.

Cleansing, that's what my heart needs
Completely, without even a trace.
My life is a canvas that He paints on
With brush strokes of mercy and grace.

Yes, come home—that great invitation
Rings out to the weary and the frail.
Come home, and fall upon the Savior
Who forgives your every betrayal.

16 Wash you, make you clean; put away the evil of your
doings from before mine eyes; cease to do evil; 17 Learn to do
well; seek judgment, relieve the oppressed, judge the father-
less, plead for the widow. 18 Come now, and let us reason
together, saith the LORD: though your sins be as scarlet,
they shall be as white as snow; though they be red like
crimson, they shall be as wool.
Isaiah 1:18

Walking Home

It is amazing how a few steps in the wrong direction so often turn into a journey of sorrow. The return to a right relationship with the Father is a wonderful thing. How truly blessed, however, are those who never leave home in the first place!

I headed out one fine day
Just to take a little walk,
And ended up with others
And we had a little talk.

We walked a ways together
And spent some time at ease,
While deciding it was best
To do just what we please.

The days just seemed to fly.
Our nights were action filled.
The flesh was always hungry
And its appetite never stilled.

The pathway that I traveled
Led me further away each day.
When my means were used up
My friends all refused to stay.

Now my life has hit the bottom
Why from my Father did I roam?
I never planned to go this far.
It's time to start walking home.

Retracing my wandering steps
On the downward slope of life,
Is a time for deep reflection
On the causes of sin and strife.

Toward Home

Each step I take on my return
Makes me long for the last mile,
When I can see forgiving arms
And His loving fatherly smile.

What a wonderful table is set
And His house has room for all.
Forgiveness is on the menu
When on His mercy we call.

11 And he said, A certain man had two sons: 12 And the
younger of them said to his father, Father, give me the
portion of goods that falleth to me. And he divided unto
them his living. 13 And not many days after the younger
son gathered all together, and took his journey into a far
country, and there wasted his substance with riotous living.
14 And when he had spent all, there arose a mighty famine
in that land; and he began to be in want. 15 And he went
and joined himself to a citizen of that country; and he sent
him into his fields to feed swine. 16 And he would fain have
filled his belly with the husks that the swine did eat: and no
man gave unto him. 17 And when he came to himself, he
said, How many hired servants of my father's have bread
enough and to spare, and I perish with hunger! 18 I will
arise and go to my father, and will say unto him, Father, I
have sinned against heaven, and before thee, 19 And am no
more worthy to be called thy son: make me as one of thy
hired servants. 20 And he arose, and came to his father. But
when he was yet a great way off, his father saw him, and
had compassion, and ran, and fell on his neck, and kissed
him. 21 And the son said unto him, Father, I have sinned
against heaven, and in thy sight, and am no more worthy
to be called thy son. 22 But the father said to his servants,
Bring forth the best robe, and put it on him; and put a
ring on his hand, and shoes on his feet: 23 And bring hither
the fatted calf, and kill it; and let us eat, and be merry: 24
For this my son was dead, and is alive again; he was lost,
and is found. And they began to be merry.

Luke 15:11~32

The Gathering

What a wonderful day it will be when the call of our Lord comes and we are taken to our eternal home in Heaven! Events of our day indicate to many that this gathering could occur at any time. Those who have not prepared spiritually for this event will not be a part of it. Have you prepared? Are you ready?

A harvest awaits its purpose,
To give a bountiful yield,
Presenting to its master
Wonderful fruits of his field.

A flock responds to the call
And turns toward the gate
Where with loving hands extended
The shepherd patiently waits.

Near the window eyes watch
As the sky begins to turn,
She moves with great dispatch
Calling little ones in concern.

A man who is set in power
With only the raising of a hand
Brings a watchful multitude
To a place where he does stand.

There is a greater gathering
Scheduled in God's plan,
When the Father of Creation
Gathers the redeemed of man.

He watches, calls, and beckons.
"Come into and under My care.
When homecoming time is come
I dearly want you to be there."

*16 For the Lord himself shall descend from heaven with a
shout, with the voice of the archangel, and with the trump
of God: and the dead in Christ shall rise first: 17 Then we
which are alive and remain shall be caught up together
with them in the clouds, to meet the Lord in the air: and so
shall we ever be with the Lord.*
I Thessalonians 4:16&17

Suppertime

Are you prepared for the call to the marriage supper of the Lamb?
We need to live as if the call of God to come home is imminent.
Many who are knowledgeable observers believe that it is.

The sun hovered low in the sky.
Daylight would soon be past.
A child plays games in the dirt.
Summer had gone by very fast.

Days were beginning to shorten.
The smell of fall was in the air.
Changes were on the horizon
But a youngster would hardly care.

A mother comes to the doorway.
Shadows will not be denied.
"It's starting to get dark, Son,
I want you to come inside.

"Come on in, get cleaned up.
Your supper is almost prepared.
Time to sit down and enjoy it.
As a family it will be shared."

If we could see heavenly events
And understand as times unfold,
We just might witness the Father
The doorknob of heaven lay hold.

Saying, "Children it is getting dark
And nighttime is on the way.
Come on home. The table is set.
Enter in now and don't delay.

"Your supper is finally ready
Get cleaned up on the way.
The feast, only the beginning
Of your eternal heavenly stay."

*7 Let us be glad and rejoice, and give honour to him: for the
marriage of the Lamb is come, and his wife hath made
herself ready. 8 And to her was granted that she should be
arrayed in fine linen, clean and white: for the fine linen is
the righteousness of saints. 9 And he saith unto me, Write,
Blessed are they which are called unto the marriage supper
of the Lamb. And he saith unto me, These are the true
sayings of God.*
Revelation 19:7-9

Standing at the Door

Distance between the Savior and His child is always a negative. Being in the family of God requires that we enter through Jesus Christ and then draw closer to and more like our Lord. Abiding sin is a great inhibitor of close fellowship and spiritual growth.

I was standing at the door
Watching the scene within.
The King beckoned me enter
And take a seat next to Him.

Knowing I was truly His Child
Adopted by faith in His Son,
You would expect me to enter
And join in the celebration.

To stand at the door I continue,
Feeling fearful to enter within.
Could it be that my hesitation
Is because of my personal sin?

Don't linger in the doorway.
My blessings you shall see,
If only you will surrender
Your stubborn will to Me.

To touch the hem of His coat,
To walk in the path He trod,
To live in the great palace,
That's close enough to God.

Oh, what blessings we miss
If satisfied with being near!
Climb up upon His great lap
Whisper and cry in His ear.

As His hand moves in your life
Gratitude will flood your soul.
You'll wonder why you waited
To make His arms your goal.

Jesus saith unto them, Come and dine. And none of the disciples durst ask him, Who art thou? knowing that it was the Lord.
John 21:12

Behold the Lamb

What a marvelous concept that God would provide His Son as the Lamb whose death would take away the sin of the world. The sin of the world concerns me, but my sin condemns me, at least until I give it all to Jesus.

Behold the Lamb of God now smitten.
See His blood flow down the tree.
He bore all my sin as it is written,
That I through Him might be set free.

Behold the Father watching this One
Stricken with grief, of sorrow no lack.
Choosing to punish His only Son,
Pouring out wrath, and turning His back.

Behold the Savior alive and well
Presenting His blood at the throne.
Victorious over the grave and hell,
The way of eternal life clearly shown.

Behold the sinner before His Lord,
As a slaughtered Lamb, You took my place.
I cling to You now by a slender chord
Made only of Your mercy and grace.

Now when the centurion, and they that were with him, watching Jesus, saw the earthquake, and those things that were done, they feared greatly, saying, Truly this was the Son of God.
Matthew 27:54

The next day John seeth Jesus coming unto him, and saith, Behold the Lamb of God, which taketh away the sin of the world.
John 1:29

Inside Actions

The Closet

God has said, in the time of trouble I will hide you in My pavilion: in the secret of My tabernacle I will hide you, I will set you up upon a rock. When things in life are rough and you don't have any answers, where are you going to run? Where are you going to hide? Why not run to your heavenly Father and the comfort and protection He offers.

I was minding my own business,
When the bad news came my way.
What would I tell my dear ones?
I couldn't think of what to say.

I examined my personal conduct,
Reviewing almost every word.
Looking for unfound answers.
How could things have occurred?

I retreated inside my closet
Both literally and in my heart.
Overwhelmed by my thoughts
Hot flowing tears were a part.

Why God, and what have I done?
Were questions that came out.
You know where my heart is
And just what I am all about.

My wife entered my closet,
Her arms brought comfort and care.
We wept and cried together,
Then our Savior met us there.

He said I know about trouble
And the fear uncertainty brings.
I will hide you in My love
And guide you in these things.

One day when this trial is past,
And you see My will in it all,
Remember the time in a closet,
When on My grace you did call.

Tell your children the story
And your grandchildren too.
Let's meet again in the closet,
I'll be there waiting for you.

*4 One thing have I desired of the LORD, that will I seek after; that I may dwell in the house of the LORD all the days of my life, to behold the beauty of the LORD, and to inquire in his temple.
5 For in the time of trouble he shall hide me in his pavilion: in the secret of his tabernacle shall he hide me; he shall set me up upon a rock.*
Psalm 27:4-5

Solitude

When you find yourself alone, it is a great time to think about God and His wonderful plan of salvation. How easy it is to push His wonderful works into rarely frequented recesses of our minds. Consider the things of God when you find yourself alone, and the fellowship will bless your soul.

Looking out on a winters night
At the freshly fallen white snow,
Considering the times of my life
And the things I ought to know.

The quietude of my surroundings
Calls my heart to search within,
For the deep truths of eternity
And their application to all men.

There was a time, there was a place,
When every creature known as man,
Has been confronted with the need
To know God's redemptive plan.

My solitude leads me to marvel
That the Savior would stand alone
And bear the sins of the world
So we might make Heaven our home.

He chose to suffer and die alone
That the guilty might be set free,
And live within the hearts of those
Who reach up to Him, just like me.

Sitting alone and considering
The wonderfulness of His love,
And the way that I discovered
The precious message from above.

My heart is filled with praise
When I think of all He has done
And that He would do no less
If I had been the only lost one.

Is your heart in need of His love?
Do you seek after inward peace?
Cast all your care upon Jesus
And you will find sweet release.

3 Thou wilt keep him in perfect peace, whose mind is stayed on thee: because he trusteth in thee. 4 Trust ye in the LORD for ever: for in the LORD JEHOVAH is everlasting strength:
Isaiah 26:3-4

Success

Successful people are just regular people who have discovered a few simple rules and follow them faithfully. In the Bible, Joshua lays it out for us very clearly. Get God's Word inside you every day and do what it says.

A wise man once said to me,
If success in life you seek,
These two things you must do,
They are simple rules to keep.

The first, a matter of your will.
You must follow directions
Knowing what is required,
Making proper corrections.

The second is about attitude
And whom you allow to rule,
Respecting your authority
Prevents your being a fool.

Living examples you will find
When you examine daily life,
That confirm these two rules
When followed, avoid strife.

As a child learns very early,
To have success in school,
One must respect authority
And submit to obey each rule.

At home with mother and father,
The rules are clearly spoken,
With loving discipline to bear
When those laws are broken.

On your job there is a boss
With authority on his side,
And he sets workplace rules
By which we all must abide.

In society, we must obey the law.
As we drive we follow a code.
Sometimes officers remind us
As they remove us from the road.

In spiritual matters indeed,
Directions must be followed.
God's word is the standard,
If His name is to be hallowed.

When at work, home or school,
Especially within the heart,
Heed authority's directions.
Today is a great day to start.

*8 This book of the law shall not depart out of thy mouth;
but thou shalt meditate therein day and night, that thou
mayest observe to do according to all that is written
therein: for then thou shalt make thy way prosperous, and
then thou shalt have good success. 9 Have not I commanded
thee? Be strong and of a good courage; be not afraid,
neither be thou dismayed: for the LORD thy God is with
thee whithersoever thou goest.*
Joshua 1:8-9

Fame

If people remember me for the spiritual qualities that have been displayed in my life, then that will mean God has worked His will in me by His Grace and eternity will have been affected in the process.

How will I be remembered,
When Jesus calls my name?
As friends and family gather,
What will be my fame?

Will I be known as a servant
Who gave each day his best,
And stood strong in adversity
While enduring every test?

What will my children say
About the way I lived my life?
Was their dad a man of God
Who honored his faithful wife?

Will they gather all around
Those I have led to the Lord,
Recognized as my true wealth
And most glorious reward?

If I have raised up Jesus
Upon the throne of my heart,
What a wonderful celebration
When time for me to depart.

A good name is rather to be chosen than great riches, and loving favour rather than silver and gold.
Proverbs 22:1

The Quiet Place

Why is it that we often avoid those things that are best for us? Spending time with God has always been a blessing to me. So why is it that I allow the little, unimportant things of life to sometimes push aside my time with God? Get to your quiet place with God whether you feel like it or not. You will never be sorry you went.

There is a quiet place,
Near to God's own heart.
Where the Spirit shows
How sin we can depart.

Come to this garden
Within the heart of man.
Walk with the Savior;
Take Him by the hand.

Be still in His presence.
Listen and you will learn
The wisdom of His council,
Great principles to discern.

The busyness of living
Makes it easy to ignore,
The call for fellowship
And an intimate rapport.

His Word opens the gate.
Its truth is the key,
To open blinded eyes
And make our spirit see.

A garden cool and fresh
Each morning does await,
Those who would avoid
Sin's ever deceiving bait.

I love them that love me; and those that seek me early shall find me.
Proverbs 8:17

The Spirit

Most of us know how to talk to God. We petition, intercede, and give thanks and praise to our Lord and Savior. Do we ever spend time in prayer and just be silent and listen with our heart? When we are as proficient at listening as we are at talking, we will hear things that we have missed in past encounters with an Almighty God.

There is a wonderful presence
The resident Spirit within,
Who counsels my inner man
And notifies me of my sin.

His work begins in my heart,
That still small voice inside,
Speaking of spiritual things
And thoughts that I try to hide.

At times my prayers need help
And I know not how to pray,
But He knows the will of God
And helps me with what to say.

He was a part of that process,
My spiritual adoption by God,
The placement into His family
From the wicked path I had trod.

He speaks not about Himself
But teaches us about God's Son,
Christ's willingness to save us
And cleanse our sins each one.

He is our wonderful counselor
But His heart can be grieved,
When we wander from the Word
And by sin we are deceived.

Success is a direct result of
Walking daily by His power,
Trusting in His leading
Every day and every hour.

Invite Him to fill your heart
And to whisper in your ear,
Guiding the steps of living
And calming all your fear.

This will result in a life
That gives praise to our Lord,
A sweet smelling sacrifice,
A beautiful heavenly chord.

26 Likewise the Spirit also helpeth our infirmities: for we know not what we should pray for as we ought: but the Spirit itself maketh intercession for us with groanings which cannot be uttered. 27 And he that searcheth the hearts knoweth what is the mind of the Spirit, because he maketh intercession for the saints according to the will of God.
Romans 8:26&27

Sacred Remembrances

Malachi tells us that those who reverenced the Lord and spoke to another about His wonderful ways caught God's ear. He goes on to say that God also recorded these things in a special book. Isn't it amazing that God's attention is turned directly on those who think about His name? These days with so many things distracting our minds, wouldn't it be wise to purposely spend time thinking about God and focusing on His goodness?

My mind calls me back
To consider once again
The wonderful works
Of my Savior and Friend.

To remember His hand
In my life and my heart,
To rejoice in His goodness
Between now and the start.

Tis wonderfully blessed
To ponder His deeds,
The provisions that came
To meet all of my needs.

Salvation, the free gift,
Then the call on my life,
And the special discovery—
God's choice for a wife.

Our children, our work,
And the way He forgives,
The power of His Word
I have seen how it lives.

Remembering to remember
Great mercy and love.
It is really a pattern
That is set from above.

The book of remembrance
Before Him made plain,
It includes each of His
Who thought on His name.

A sacred remembrance
We must never forsake.
Considering His ways
Our praises we make.

Then they that feared the LORD spake often one to another: and the LORD hearkened, and heard it, and a book of remembrance was written before him for them that feared the LORD, and that thought upon his name.
Malachi 3:16

A Bad Day

The landscape of our daily existence is affected by our focus. Looking at life from strictly my point of view breeds selfishness, sorrow, and dreary days. Looking up through God's word and prayer allows the Son to shine all the time.

I was having a perfectly bad day.
Then Jesus came and ruined it all.
He said it wasn't His plan for me.
No, that wasn't a part of His call.

I was having a perfectly lost soul,
When He first came into my life,
And gave me something to live for,
To escape from eternal strife.

I was enjoying an evil thought,
Hatred and revenge combined,
Jesus came along and spoiled it.
His love converted my mind.

I was having a total pity party.
Someone had treated me wrong.
He showed me a glimpse of Calvary
As He hung before the throng.

I was developing a selfish idea
"Me first" sounded just right.
When Jesus said to my heart,
"Humility will bring you light."

I was happy with my witness
You know, the lifestyle kind.
Jesus said, "Speak up about Me,
And salvation they will find."

Inside Actions

I was having a conversation.
Just the facts if you will.
Jesus said, "Hold your tongue.
Let gossiping lips be still."

I had given my word to help,
I just couldn't keep it, you see.
Jesus reminded me of His Word—
The importance of integrity.

I was feeling pretty righteous
When Jesus looked deep inside.
Oh, what a great revelation,
All the secrets I tried to hide.

Now I have perfectly good days
When His Holy Word I read,
And draw on its power daily,
Then follow His every lead.

Thy word is a lamp unto my feet, and a light unto my path.
Psalm 119:105

Obedience

How easy it is to please God by simply saying yes to Him. How often we do the opposite and lose the peace and blessings He offers. If even the elements of this world obey Him, why won't we?

Some say the wind is free
To blow just any which way,
But when the Master speaks
Even the winds must obey.

The sea directs its current
And sends it where it will,
But when the Master speaks
The mighty waves are still.

The Savior spoke his name.
Immediately he did obey,
And left his gravely prison
To live for another day.

Are we any less responsible
Than death, the wave, the wind,
To obey the Master's will
Whose Son to Calvary did send?

Lord, please help me to obey
From out of a grateful heart.
Defeat the resistant spirit
That beckons me to depart.

And as creation around me
Heeds Your every command,
A wandering heart is fettered
When in Your strength I stand.

39 And he arose, and rebuked the wind, and said unto the sea, Peace, be still. And the wind ceased, and there was a great calm. 41 And they feared exceedingly, and said one to another, What manner of man is this, that even the wind and the sea obey him?
Mark 4:35~41

My Friend

Written in remembrance of a Godly man, L.C. Pinnegar, whose children and grandchildren are actively seeking to walk with God in their lives. Does this remind you of someone you have known and loved? If it does, you are truly blessed.

Today, my friend of many years
Received his calling home.
The way provided by his Lord
On a path so clearly shown.

He loved me; he loved each one.
His heart had room for all.
Strength displayed when needed,
And spiritually, he stood tall.

He called me to his bedside,
With others, both young and old.
"Live right and don't let go
Of the things you've been told."

My friend is home with Jesus.
His great concern and care
Was that the steps be taken
To, one day, join him there.

And devout men carried Stephen to his burial, and made great lamentation over him.
Acts 8:2

My Treasure

When God has melded two lives together through marriage, children and many wonderful years, the separation that comes in the death of a beloved partner is one of the most painful experiences that could ever be endured. Those of us who have not walked this path cannot truly understand the pain of those who have. There is One who does know our grief and broken heart, and when we release our loved one to His care we know they are eternally blessed. Letting go—sounds easy, but many can testify how hard it really is to do. If you know people who have experienced this type of loss, bless their hearts by remembering to pray for them and remember to contact them from time to time, and check on how they are getting along.

God has given me a treasure
In an earthen vessel contained,
Today I must surrender her
For heaven she has gained.

The things we shared together
The joy, the pain, the tears,
Two living, yet really one—
How fleeting are the years.

Long ago she opened her heart
To the Savior she has gone to see,
She gave immeasurable gifts—
Our children, our family.

Lord, I've been forced to let go
Of the treasure that You gave,
And entrust her care to You
As the One who came to save.

She was a wonderful gift,
A true blessing to my life.
Thank You for this treasure.
Thank You for my loving wife.

In loving memory of
Esther Spurlock

10 Who can find a virtuous woman? for her price is far above
rubies. 11 The heart of her husband doth safely trust in her, so
that he shall have no need of spoil. 12 She will do him good and
not evil all the days of her life. 13 She seeketh wool, and flax,
and worketh willingly with her hands. 14 She is like the mer-
chants' ships; she bringeth her food from afar. 15 She riseth also
while it is yet night, and giveth meat to her household, and a
portion to her maidens. 16 She considereth a field, and buyeth it:
with the fruit of her hands she planteth a vineyard. 17 She
girdeth her loins with strength, and strengtheneth her arms. 18
She perceiveth that her merchandise is good: her candle goeth
not out by night. 19 She layeth her hands to the spindle, and
her hands hold the distaff. 20 She stretcheth out her hand to
the poor; yea, she reacheth forth her hands to the needy. 21 She
is not afraid of the snow for her household: for all her house-
hold are clothed with scarlet. 22 She maketh herself coverings of
tapestry; her clothing is silk and purple. 23 Her husband is
known in the gates, when he sitteth among the elders of the
land. 24 She maketh fine linen, and selleth it; and delivereth
girdles unto the merchant. 25 Strength and honour are her
clothing; and she shall rejoice in time to come. 26 She openeth
her mouth with wisdom; and in her tongue is the law of
kindness. 27 She looketh well to the ways of her household, and
eateth not the bread of idleness. 28 Her children arise up, and
call her blessed; her husband also, and he praiseth her. 29
Many daughters have done virtuously, but thou excellest them
all. 30 Favour is deceitful, and beauty is vain: but a woman
that feareth the LORD, she shall be praised. 31 Give her of the
fruit of her hands; and let her own works praise her in the
gates.

Poem Index